Vaping Home Brewers Handbook
Volume 1

Vaping Home Brewers Handbook
Volume 1

Damien Smy

Vaping Home Brewers Publishing
2016

Dedication

This book is dedicated to my loving family, and my friends on Facebook. Without their help, input, and advice, I never would have gotten this project to where it is today.

Contents

Acknowledgements

I would like to thank the Admins and members of Vaping Home Brewers for their feedback, recipes, tips, tricks and advice. Without the Vaping Home Brewers group and members, this series of books would not exist.

I would also like to thank Alex Mackz of MackzDesignz for the amazing artwork on the cover.

Foreword

My own mixing journey has been a somewhat slow and painful one I was mistaken in the early days, believing that you could just buy any ingredients and literally throw them together, as a result my mixes were somewhat dire and mostly unvapeable.

However I did become frustrated by my lack of results and decided the only real way to tackle the issue was by full research, several years later I am now producing quality juices for myself, close friends and vaping family members

The recipes contained in this publication are sourced from many places ,so credit needs to be given for those who put the groundwork in on developing the recipes and a big thanks for being willing to share with the vaping public

Credit also goes to the concentrate manufacturers for their development of concentrates suitable for the production of safe e-liquids. Lastly but not least credit goes to the people involved in making this publication available to us,and to the members of Vaping Home brewers for the interest they have shown in the group and their willingness to share their knowledge.

Kal Morris

Preface

The Vaping Home Brewers Handbook began life as a few files on a Facebook group. The next stage in their life, the recipes were pretty much copied and pasted into the Vaping Home Brewers Recipe Collection, Volume 1.

Formatting was poor, spelling was awful, yet, it managed to do it's job, and revitalise the way the group files were being used. A flurry of recipes followed, more than trebling the content, so Volume 2 was created.

Now, we are attempting to ensure an easier view and mixing experience by formatting everything in a consistent and uniform manner.

I hope you enjoy the work of a dedicated core of people.

Introduction

Throughout the book, you will see a reference to steeping times, and these times will be condensed after each chapter into a table. Some recipes do not state steeping times. The reason for this is because the developer did not state the time when they posted the recipe to the group.

You can follow a basic guideline for certain types of recipe however, just take a look at the ingredients, and refer to the following table based on the content.

This table does not replace the advice of the creator. A full guide to steeping e-liquids can be found at the rear of the book, in the Appendix Chapters.

Recipe Type	Steeping Time
Fruit	7-10 Days
Custard	28 Days
Yoghurt/Cream	14-21 Days
Chocolate/Coffee	21-28 Days
Tobacco	7-14 Days
Mint/Menthol	2-7 Days

Drink or Alcohol Style Recipes

VANILLA CHAI LATTE
FA Black Tea 1-2%
FA Vienna Cream 1%
FA Vanilla Tahiti 0.5%
FA Cardamon 0.5%
FA Cinnamon 0.5%
FA Anise 0.5%
FA Clove 0.5%
FA Honey 0.15%

....

POMEGANITE CHERRYADE
TFA Black Cherry 2%
LO Cherry 6%
LO Pomegranate 7%
TFA Sweetener 3.5%
LO Tart and Sour 1.5%

....

APRICOT BRANDY
TFA Apricot 9%
TFA/FW Brandy 5%
TFA/FW Honey 2%
TFA Lemon 1%
TFA Sweetener 3%

....

SUMMERADE
TFA Watermelon (TFA) 10%
TFA Mango (TFA) 8%
INA Lemon (INA) 3%
FW Lemonade (FW) 5%
Note: If you want a cooling sensation add some TFA Koolada 0.5%-1.5%

....

IRISH CREAM MILKSHAKE
FA Irish Cream 0.5%
FA Fresh Cream 0.5%
FA Caramel 0.5%
FA Vienna Cream 0.5%

....

RASPBERRY LEMONADE
TPA Lemon 7%
CK Raspberry 8%
Ethyl Maltol 10% Solution 0.5%

....

ICY BLUE
CK Raspberry 13%
TFA Blueberry Wild 4%
TFA Citrus Punch 1%
TFA Menthol 1%-1.5% According To Taste

....

CHERRY AMERETTO
LO Cherry 9%
LO Amaretto 9%
Sweeten To Taste
7 Day Steep

....

TASTY STRAWBERRY MILKSHAKE
CAP Strawberries And Cream 4%
CAP Sweet Strawberry 3%
TFA Strawberry 3%
TFA Ripe Strawberry 3%
CAP Vanilla Custard V2 2%
14 Day Steep

....

RIGHTWAY
TFA Absinthe 2%
TFA Irish Cream 6%
TFA Green Apple 6%
TFA Toasted Almond 2%
FW/INA Whiskey 2%
FA Bitter Wizard 2%

....

STRAWBERRY SODA
TFA Cola 7%
LO Strawberry 11%
TFA Sweetener 3.5%
3 Day Steep

....

STRAWBERRY LIMEADE
FA Lemon Sicily 1%
FA Lime Cold-Pressed 3%
TFA Strawberry Ripe 4%
2 Day Steep

....

HARD LEMONADE
LO Lemonade 6 %
TFA Kentucky Bourbon 3 %
TFA Vanillin 10% Solution 2 %
10 Day Steep

....

XTREME COLA
TFA Cola 8%
TFA Cinnamon Spice 4%
TFA Bavarian Cream 4%
TFA Sweetener 3.5%
12 Hour Breathe
10 Day Steep

....

VIMTOISH
TPA Gummy Candy 7%
TPA Grape 7%
Ethyl Maltol 2 Drops Per 10ml
24 Hour Breathe
7 Day Steep

....

KARAKOF CREAM (Creamy Caramel Coffee)
TPA Bavarian Cream 2.5%
FW Coffee with Cream 7%
FW Caramel Candy 5%
14 Day Steep

....

BANANA MILKSHAKE
TPA Ripe Banana 5%
TPA Graham Cracker 4%
TPA Malted Milk 9%
TPA Vanilla Bean Ice Cream 4%
TPA Koolada 2 Drops Per 10ml
....

CHAMPERS
TFA Champagne 10%
TFA Strawberry Ripe 6%
TFA Juicy Peach 4%
....

Vaping Home Brewers Handbook

Flavour	Steeping Time
Cherry Ameretto	7 Days
Tasty Strawberry Milkshake	14 Days
Strawberry Soda	3 Days
Strawberry Limeade	2 Days
Hard Lemonade	10 Days
Xtreme Cola	10 Days
Vimtoish	7 Days
Karakof Cream	14 Days

Fruit or Fruity Style Recipes

STRAWBERRY AND BANANA
INA Strawberry 3%
INA Banana 3%

....

BANGIN' ORANGE
FW Orange 8%
TPA Sweet Cream 5%
CAP Sweet Tangerine 8%

....

SUMMER VAPE
LO Banana Cream 7%
TPA Coconut 4%
TPA Dragonfruit 4%
TPA Pineapple 2%
TPA Strawberry 4%

....

PEARNANA By Kal Morris
TPA Pear 8%
TPA Banana Cream 8%
3 Day Steep

....

WILD BUNCH
TFA Blueberry Wild 5%
CAP Marshmallow 2.5%
TFA Sweetener 2.5%
FW Wild Cherry 5%
INA Wild Strawberry 5%

....

PEAR TWIST
TFA Pear 10%
TFA Bavarian Cream 5%
TFA Coconut Extra 2%
TFA Sweet Cream 2%
TFA Apricot 1%

....

APPLE ICE
TFA Apple 16%
TFA Menthol 3%
ANY Ethyl Maltol 10% Solution 1%

....

SIN CITY
TFA Apple 8%
TFA Watermelon 5%
FW Jolly Rancher 6%

....

ANGEL
TFA Dulce de Leche 2%
TFA New York Cheesecake 4%
TFA Sweet Strawberry 7%
TFA Raspberry 2%
TFA Peach 3%
TFA Ethyl Maltol 10% Solution 1.2%
TFA Smooth 1%

....

THE KALSTER'S DELIGHT
CAP Blue Raspberry Cotton Candy 6%
CAP Passionfruit 5%
CAP Grapefruit 4%
CAP Lemon Sicily 5%

....

TROPICAL COOLER
TFA Mango 6%
TFA Passionfruit 5%
TFA Pineapple 3%
INA Menthol 0.8%

....

HEAVEN CAN WAIT
ANY Ethyl Maltol 10% Solution 1.5%
FW Key Lime 3%
FA Lime Tahiti 2%
TPA Nectarine 4%
CAP Strawberries and Cream 4%
CAP Sweet Strawberry 5%

....

ORANGE WITH A TWIST
TPA Bavarian Cream 3%
TPA Cotton Candy 2%
FA MTS Vape Wizard 0.5%
TFA Orange Mandarin 5%
CAP Orange Mango 4%
TPA Sour 0.5%
ANY Stevia Sweetener 0.5%
TPA Strawberry Ripe 4%

....

BLUEBERRY BOOGER
CAP or CK Blueberry 8%
FW Acai 4%

....

CRYSTAL LITE
TFA Coconut 6.5%
TFA Pineapple 3%
TFA Coconut Candy 2%
TFA Golden Pineapple 4%
TFA Pear 2.5%
TFA Whipped Cream 2%
10 Day Steep

....

KALBERRY
LO Blueberry 6%
TFA Cranberry 4%
LO Raspberry 4%
LO Strawberry 5%
TFA Sweet Cream 2%
Sweeten To Taste

....

BSC
CAP Banana 8%
CAP Strawberries & Cream 6%

....

MELON CHILL Posted By Lee Scaife
TPA Watermelon 8%
CAP Honeydew 8%
CAP Peppermint 2%
TFA Koolada 2%
ANY Ethyl Maltol 10% Solution 2%
2 Day Steep

....

WHITE CHOCOLATE ORANGE By Joseph Francis
CAP Vanilla Bean Ice Cream 10%
TPA Orange Cream 4%
TPA White Chocolate 3%
CAP Vanilla Custard V1 1%
TPA Whipped Cream 2%

....

STRAWPEARY
TFA Honeydew 3%
TFA Strawberry Ripe 3%
TFA Pear 6%
12 Hour Breathe
1 Day Steep

....

CREAMY MANGO AND PINEAPPLE
TPA Bavarian Cream 5%
FW Mango 5%
FA Pineapple 3%
CAP Vanilla Cupcake 1.5%
14 Day Steep

....

GONE BANANAS
LO Banana 6 %
FW/CAP Banana 5%
TFA Ripe Banana 4%
TFA Sweetener 3.5%
24 Hour Breathe
2 Day Steep

....

WILD BUNCH
TFA Blueberry Wild 5%
CAP Marshmallow 2.5%
TFA Sweetener 2.5%
FW Wild Cherry 5%
INA Wild Strawberry 5%
24 Hour Breathe
7 Day Steep

....

RED ,BLUE AND PEACHY
TFA Peach Juicy 6%
TFA Blueberry Extra 6%
TFA Strawberry Ripe 6%
24 Hour Breathe
7 Day Steep

....

STRANGELY STRAWBERRY
CAP Cucumber 0.3%
FA Strawberry 1.25%
CAP Sweet Strawberry 7.5%
12 Hour Breathe
1 Day Steep

....

BERRY MEDLEY YOGHURT
TFA Blue Raspberry 3.5%
TFA Blueberry Extra 3.5%
TFA Strawberry Ripe 3.5%
TFA Bavarian Cream 2%
CAP Vanilla Custard v2 2%
TFA Sweetener 2%
TFA Vanilla Swirl 2%
TFA Yogurt Flavour 5%
28-42 Day Steep

....

PINEAPPLE CREAM
TFA Whipped Cream 3%
TFA Sweet Cream 5%
CAP golden pineapple 11%
24 Hour Breathe
10 Day Steep

....

COOL BANANA
TFA Koolada 0.50%
FW Banana 4%
CAP Banana 8%
TFA Marshmallow 2%
24 Hour Breathe
10 Day Steep

....

BANGIN' ORANGE
CAP Orange 7%
CAP Sweet Tangerine 8%
KH Orange Tick Tac 2 %
TPA Sweet Cream 3%
14 Day Steep

....

VACATION MIX
CAP Golden Pineapple 2.5%
TFA Kiwi Double 2%
TFA Green Apple 1.5%
TFA Dragonfruit 3%
CAP Guava 2%
TFA Pina Colada Flavour 7%
24 Hour Breathe
2 Day Steep
....

CHERRY SUGAR
TFA Sweet Raspberry 1%
TFA Sour 1%
FW Blueberry Cotton Candy 4%
DV Sour Cherry 5%
....

JUICY FRUIT CHEWING GUM Posted By Joe Nukem
TFA Pineapple 10%
CAP Banana 10%
2-3 Day Steep
....

BANGIN' BANANA MILK
TPA Ripe Banana 5%
TPA Graham Cracker 4%
TPA Malted Milk 8%
TPA Vanilla Bean Ice Cream 6%
....

VOODOO
TFA Sweetener 3.5%
TFA Juicy Peach Flavour 11%
TFA Raspberry Sweet 5%
24 Hour Breathe
2 Day Steep
....

STRAWBERRY AND BANANA SMOOTHIE
TPA Banana Cream 9%
TPA Ripe Strawberry 8%
TPA Sweet Cream 3%
TPA Dairy Milk 1%

....

HULDRA
FW Acai 4.5 %
FW Blueberry 4.5%
FW Blackberry 4.5%
FW Mango 2%
FW Pomegranate 4.5%

....

STRAWBERRY DRAGON
TPA Bavarian Cream 2%
FW Dragonfruit 8%
TPA Ethyl Maltol 10% Solution 1%
TPA Koolada 1%
CAP Strawberry Sweet 5%
TPA Vanilla Swirl 1%
TPA Whipped Cream 1%

....

KAL'S KANDY
TFA Cantaloupe 2%
FA Custard 1.25%
FA Papaya 1%
FA Mango 0.5%
FA Strawberry 1%
FA Kiwi 0.5%
Sweeten To Taste

....

RED PUNCH
CAP Grenadine 3%
TFA Dragonfruit 3%
CAP Blackberry 2%
TFA Blackcurrant 3%
TFA Hawaiian Punch 3%
TFA Sweetener 3%

....

Flavour	Steeping Time
Pearnana	3 Days
Triple Melon Mix	7 Days
Crystal Lite	10 Days
Melon Chilli	2 Days
Strawpeary	1 Day
Creamy Mango and Pineapple	14 Days
Gone Bananas	2 Days
Wild Bunch	7 Days
Red, Blue, and Peachy	7 Days
Berry Medley Yoghurt	42 Days
Pineapple Cream	10 Days
Bangin' Orange	14 Days
Vacation Mix	2 Days
Juicy Fruit Chewing Gum	3 Days

Flavour	Steeping Time
Voodoo	2 Days

EXPLOSION
FW Strawberry 7.5%
FW Milk 4%
FW Vanilla Cup Cake 6%
FW Fruit Rings 4.5%

....

CRUNCHBERRIES posted by Ash Ley
TPA Strawberry Ripe 10%
TPA Cheesecake Graham Crust 5%
TPA Bavarian Cream 6%
TPA French Vanilla Deluxe 2%
7 Day Steep
Originally found on reddit

....

STRAWBERRY YOGURT
CAP Creamy Yogurt 5%
CAP Sweet Strawberry 4%
TFA Strawberry Ripe 4%
FA Meringue 0.5%
FA Caramel 0.5%
TFA/CAP Ethyl Maltol 10% Solution 1%

....

HONEY NUT CHEERIOS
FW Hazelnut 2%
FA Meringue 1.5%
FW Yellow Cake 2%
FA Marzipan 2%
TFA Acetyl Pyrazine 0.7%
FA Honey 0.4%
FW Milk 2%
TFA Almond Amaretto 1%
TFA Strawberry Ripe 2%
TFA Sweetener 1%

....

Flavour	Steeping Time
Crunchberries	7 Days

Shake and Vape Recipes

BAT JUICE
VV Bat Juice 15%
70/30 VG/PG
Left With Lid Off Overnight And Shake Well In Morning

....

STRAWKIWI By William Cannon
TFA Kiwi 2.5%
TFA Strawberry 2%
Shake And Vape Is Good But Better After 1 Night Left Open To
Breathe

....

AFRO RED Jennie Bell
TFA Red Astaire 10%
TFA Afro Dizziac 3%
24 Hour Breathe But Can Shake And Vape!

....

COOLBERRY ByJennie Bell
TFA Blackcurrant 10%
TFA Raspberry 6%
TFA Mentol 2%

....

Dessert Style Recipes

BLUE CUSTARD
TPA Vanilla Custard 6%
TPA Blueberry Wild 6%
TPA Vanilla Swirl 4%
TPA Bavarian Cream 3%
TPA Sweetener 1%
28 Day Steep

....

CASTLEBROSIA AMBROSIA CLONE
CAP Cinnamon Danish Swirl 12%
TPA Vanilla Cupcake 2%
TPA Sweet Cream 2%
Sweeten To Taste.
14 Day Steep

....

STRAWBERRY BANANA CHEESECAKE Posted by: Poyn2Ohmyvayp
TFA Banana Cream 5%
TFA Strawberry Ripe 5%
TFA Cheesecake Graham Crust 8%
FW Whipped Cream 3%
ANY Ethyl Maltol 10% Solution 1%

....

VANILLA ICE CREAM by Michael Lead
FW Kool Effects 1%
CAP French Vanilla 8%
CAP Sweet Cream 10%
FW Marshmallow 11%
CAP Coconut 6%

....

GRANTS VANILLA CUSTARD - (a different approach)
CAP French Vanilla 3%
CAP New York Cheesecake 3%
CAP Vanilla Custard v1 4%
ANY Ethyl Maltol 10% Solution 1%

....

KEY LIME PIE
TFA Key Lime 12%
TFA Caramel Original 2%
TFA Vanilla Bourbon 2%
TFA Sweetener 1%
Lime Juice 1%

....

STRAWBERRY CHEESECAKE
CAP New York Cheesecake 14%
CAP Sweet Strawberry 7%
CAP Marshmallow 1%
Citric Acid or Lemon Juice 1%
ANY Ethyl Maltol 10% Solution 2%

....

RASPBERRY BASTARD
CAP Raspberry 8%
CAP Vanilla Custard v1 6%
CAP Chocolate Glazed Doughnut 3%
CAP Sweet Strawberry 2%
FA Vape Wizard 1%

....

APRICOT PIE
CAP Apricot 2%
TFA Almond 1%
CAP Cinnamon Danish Swirl 1%
TFA Whipped Cream 1%
TFA Vanillin 1%
TFA Graham Cracker 0.5%
FA White Peach 0.5%
FA Cinnamon Ceylon 0.5%
ANY Ethyl Maltol 10% Solution 1%

....

GABBON
TFA Apple Pie 9%
TFA Vanilla Bean Ice Cream 5%
TFA Caramel 2.5%
TFA Cotton Candy 1.5%
TFA Bavarian Cream 1%
TFA Graham Cracker 0.8%

....

PARK AVENUE VANILLA CHEESECAKE
CAP New York Cheesecake 10%
CAP French Vanilla 5%

....

BUTTERSCOTCH DELIGHT
FW Butterscotch 8%
FW Caramel 3%
FW Fresh Cream 3%

....

RASPBERRY CUSTARD
CAP Vanilla Custard v1 11%
CAP Raspberry 6.5%
ANY Ethyl Maltol 10% Solution 0.3%

....

PEACH COFFEE CAKE
TFA Juicy Peach 10%
CAP Cinnamon Coffee Cake 2%
TFA Toasted Marshmallow 2%

....

LEMON MERINGUE PIE
FA Lemon Sicily 4%
FA Custard 2%
FA Meringue 1%
FA Fresh Cream 0.5%
FA Apple Pie 0.5%
FA Cookie 0.5%
FA Lime Cold Pressed 0.5%

....

BANOFEE
FA Banana 8%
LO English Toffee 7%

....

CHOCCY CUSTARD
CAP Vanilla Custard V1 11%
TFA Toasted Marshmallow 4%
TFA Milk Chocolate 5%
TFA Chocolate 5%

....

APPLE PIE DELUXE
TFA Apple Pie 12%
TFA French Vanilla Deluxe 3%
TFA Whipped Cream 2%
TFA Caramel 2%
Ethyl Maltol 10% Solution 1%

....

BAVARIAN CUSTARD
TPA Bavarian Cream 5%
FW Pralines and Cream 4%
CAP Vanilla Custard v2 5%

....

MOMS PINEAPPLE CAKE
CAP Cake Batter 3%
TPA Graham Cracker 3%
CAP New York Cheesecake 2%
TPA Pineapple 2%
CAP Vanilla Custard v1 4%

....

APPLES AND DIP CLONE
FW Butterscotch 8%
FA Fuji Apple 10%
ANY Ethyl Maltol 10% Solution 1%

....

VANILLA CUSTARD
CAP Vanilla Custard v1 9%
TFA Smooth 2%
TFA Bavarian Cream 2%
TFA Graham Cracker 1.5%
FA Catalan Cream 1%
CAP Butter 1%
LO Eggnog 1%
....

WHITE S'MORES
TFA Toasted Marshmallow 6.75%
FW White Chocolate 5%
TFA Vanilla Bean 3%
TFA Sweetener 1%
FW Butterscotch 0.5%
....

TWINKIE
FW Yellow Cake 4%
TFA Vanilla Cupcake 5%
TFA Bavarian Cream 3%
TFA Sweet Cream 3%
TFA Sweetener 3%
....

CREAMY CARAMEL
CAP Marshmallow 2%
FW Dulce de Leche 2%
FW Salted Caramel 5%
24 Hour Breathe
10 Day Steep
....

PINEAPPLE CHEESECAKE
TFA French Vanilla 1%
CAP Golden Pineapple 5%
FA Vienna Cream 2%
CAP New York Cheesecake 4%
Sweeten To Taste
21 Day Steep
....

RED EYE
TFA Bavarian Cream 2%
CAP vanilla custard v1 7%
CAP sweet strawberry 1.5%
Ethyl Maltol 10% Solution 1 drop per 10ml
....

CHARLAS MILK
TFA Strawberry Ripe 9%
TFA Bavarian Cream 3%
TFA Vanilla Custard 3%
TFA Cheesecake Graham Crust 2%
TFA Sweet Cream 3%
....

BLACK FOREST CAKE
CAP Jamaican Rum 1%
CAP Vanilla Custard v2 2%
TFA Double Chocolate Clear 5%
TFA Whipped Cream 8%
TFA Maraschino Cherry 4.5%
14 Day Steep
....

BENDRO'S STRAWBERRY HORCHATA:
TFA Sweet Cream 5%
TFA Vanilla Bean Ice Cream 4%
TFA DX Vanilla Cupcake 3%
TFA Strawberry 2%
TFA Marshmallow 2%
TFA Horchata 1%
FW Madagascar Vanilla 1%
....

Flavour	Steeping Time
Blue Custard	28 Days
Cattlebrosia	14 Days
Sweet Honey Waffles	14 Days
Creamy Caramel	10 Days
Pineapple Cheesecake	21 Days
Black Forest Cake	14 Days

Tobacco Style Recipes

SMOKING SNAKE
TFA Honeydew 2.5%
TFA RY4 Double 2.5%
TFA Bavarian Cream 5%
TFA Pear 7%
5 Day Steep

....

COFFEE AND A SMOKE!
LO Keoke Coffee 4%
TPA RY4 4%
TPA Toasted Almond 2%
ANY Tobacco Absolute 3.5%

....

CHRIS' PUB VAPE:
FA Golden Rollie 3%
FA Fuji Apple 0.5%
TPA Bavarian Cream 2%
TPA Caramel 2%

....

GINGERBREAD BACKY By Martin Hinchliffe
FA Golden Rollie 2%
CAP Gingerbread 5%
MTS Vape Wizard 1%
10 Day Steep

....

Flavour	Steeping Time
Smoking Snake	5 Days
Gingerbread Backy	10 Days

Miscellaneous Recipes

THE TIDES OF MARCH
PS Rip Tide 10%
TFA Grape Candy 4%
KH Blue Raspberry 3%
CAP Blue Cotton Candy 2%
INA Menthol 1%

....

PURPLE BEAR
TFA Grape Juice 12%
TFA Gummy Candy 8%
TFA Koolada 1.5%

....

DRUMMER GIRL
FA Vanilla Tahiti 1%
FA Jamaican Rum 1%
FA Jasmine 1%
FA Ylang Ylang 0.5%
FA Caramel 0.25%

....

A PAIR OF DRAGONS
TFA Pear 7%
TFA Marshmallow 4%
TFA Sweet Cream 3%
TFA Dragonfruit 4%
TFA Bavarian Cream 1%
TFA French Vanilla 1%
21-28 Day Steep

....

JABBA JUICE
FA Pear 6%
TFA Ripe Strawberry 5%
TFA Ripe Banana 3%
TFA Sour 1%
TFA Sweet Cream 1%
TFA Marshmallow 1%
TFA Honeydew 1%
TFA Banana Cream 0.5%
TFA Juicy Peach 0.5%

....

GRAND MARINER
FA Brandy 2%
FA Orange 1.5%
FA Bergamot 1.5%
FA Custard 1.5%
FA Fresh Cream 0.5%

....

FREYA
CAP-Sweet Strawberry 9%
CK-Blueberry 8%
TFA-Sweet Cream 3%
TFA-Dulce de Leche 2%
TFA-Vanilla Swirl 1%
Ethyl Maltol 10% Solution 1%

....

SMARTIES SHELL
TPA Strawberry 6%
TPA Tutti Frutti 6%
TPA Sweet Tarts 4%
TPA Sour 4%
40/60 VG/PG

....

TOFFEE APPLE
LO Apple 8%
FW Caramel Candy 6%
TPA/TFA Caramel 6%

....

SNOW BALLS
TFA Menthol 2%
ANY Vanilla Custard 3%
TFA Peppermint 6%
....

BLACK MENTHOL By Kal Morris
FA Blackcurrant 8%
FA Liquorice 2%
FA Menthol Artic 2%
....

GREEN GIRL
FA Fuji Apple 6.5%
FA Vanilla 1.75%
FA Coconut 3.25%
....

SKITTLES
FW Skits Candy 7.5%
TFA Rainbow Drops 7.5%
TFA Cotton Candy 1.5%
LO Tart and Sour 0.5%
TFA Sweetener 3%
10 Day Steep
....

BANANA NUT BREAD
TFA French Vanilla 5.5%
TFA Banana Nut Bread 16.5%
2 Day Steep
....

SWEDISH FISH
FW Swedish Fish 7.5%
TFA Swedish Gummy 7.5%
TFA Cotton Candy 1.5%
TFA Sweetener 3.5%
10 Day Steep
....

KALSTER VAPES ICE ICE BABY
TFA Koolada 2%
TFA Menthol 2%
TFA Peppermint 10%
2 Day Steep

....

PEANUT BUTTER SURPRISE
TFA Toasted Marshmallow 2%
LA Peanut Butter 10%
10 Day Steep

....

TRIX
TFA Lemon Lime 0.30%
TFA Cheesecake Graham Crust 0.60%
TFA Malted Milk Extra 1.5 %
TFA Sweet Cream 5%
TFA Cotton Candy 3%
TFA Strawberry 5%
TFA Blueberry Wild 5%

....

GRINGO
TFA Cinnamon Spice 1%
TFA Horchata Smooth 6%
TFA Malted Milk 2%
TFA Sweetener 3%
TFA Vanilla Swirl 3%

....

MAN FLU CLONE
CV Honey and Lemon Menthol 15%
TFA Menthol 1%
TFA Absinthe 0.75%

....

CINNAMON TOAST CRUNCH By Tim Clinard
CAP Cinnamon Danish Swirl V2 10%
TFA Hazelnut 1.5%
TFA Malted Milk 4%
TFA Sweetener 4%

....

LOVERS ROCK By vapechick at dot1ml.com
FA Cinnamon Ceylon 10%
TFA Vanilla Cupcake 5%
FW Sweet Cream 5%

....

KALSTER VAPES BUTTEFRSCOTCH CUSTARD
TPA Butterscotch 7%
TPA Toasted Marshmallow 2%
TPA Brown Sugar Extra 1%
FA Caramel 2%
CAP Vanilla Custard V1 4%
TPA Bavarian Cream 2%

....

BLACKOUT
TFA Peanut Butter 8%
TFA Bavarian Cream 2%
TFA Graham Cracker 3%
TFA Brown Sugar Extra 1%
FW Hazelnut 1%
FA Caramel 1%
FA Torrone 0.25%

....

SINFUL CHERRY CREAM
TFA Sweet Cream 6%
TFA Black Cherry 5%
TFA Bavarian Cream 4%
TFA Vanilla Bean Ice Cream 2%
TFA Maraschino Cherry 1%
TFA Smooth 1%

....

LOFN (Goddess Of Forbidden Love)
TFA Absinthe 10%
TFA Koolada 1%
TFA Peppermint 4%
Ethyl Maltol 10% Solution 2 Drops Per 10Ml

....

TRUE BLOOD
TFA Strawberry 6%
TFA White Chocolate 9%
TFA Sweet Cream 2%
TFA Ethyl Maltol 10% Solution 3%

....

Vaping Home Brewers Handbook

Flavour	Steeping Time
A Pair of Dragons	28 Days
Skittles	10 Days
Swedish Fish	10 Days
Ice Ice Baby	2 Days
Peanut Butter Surprise	10 Days
Cool Monster	7 Days

Clone Recipes

GAMBIT CLONE
TFA Apple Pie 13.5%
TFA Pie Crust 5%
TFA French Vanilla Deluxe 4%
TFA Whipped Cream 3%
TFA Caramel 2%

....

SUICIDE BUNNY ORIGINAL BUNNY CLONE
TFA Vanilla Custard 10%
CAP Cake Batter 7%
TFA Sweet Cream 4%
TFA Bavarian Cream 4%

....

MOTHER'S MILK CLONE
CAP Cake Batter 3%
CAP Sweet Strawberry 15%
FW Bavarian Cream 3.5%
TFA Ethyl Maltol 10% Solution 1.5%
FA Smooth 1%
FA Magic Mask 1%
14 Day Steep

....

BETTY CLONE
FW Strawberry 5%
FW Pear 2%
FW Kiwi 3%
FW Pineapple 2%
FW Cantaloupe 2%
FW Guava 2%
FW Grapefruit 1%
FW Watermelon 2%
FW Peach 1%
TFA Smooth 2%

....

SNICKER DOODLE COOKIE CLONE
TFA Cinnamon Danish 8%
TFA Cinnamon Sugar Cookie 6%
FA Vanilla Tahiti 2%
TFA Sweet Cream 2%
TFA Toasted Almond 1%
70/30 or 60/40 VG/PG

....

PAPA SMURF CLONE
TFA Pomegranate Deluxe 7%
CK Blueberry 8%
TFA Sweet Cream 3%
Ethyl Maltol 10% Solution 2%

....

ROSTA BLOOD CLONE
TFA Strawberries and Cream 5%
TFA Strawberry 4%
TFA White Chocolate 8%
TFA Mary Jane 4%

....

COSMIC FOG MILK AND HONEY
TFA Graham Cracker Clear 5%
TFA Marshmallow 2%
TFA Vanilla Swirl 2%
CAP Vanilla Custard v1 2%
TFA Peanut Butter 1.4%

....

8 BALL CLONE
TFA Banana Ripe 4%
TFA Caramel Original 3%
FA Expresso 2%
TFA Sweet Cream 3%

....

5 PAWNS QUEENSIDE CLONE
TFA French Vanilla 10%
TFA Orange Cream 10%
TFA Koolada 1%

....

BLUE VOODOO FROM MISTER ELIQUID CLONE
TFA Juicy Peach 10%
TFA Sweet Raspberry 5%
TFA Sweetener 5%

....

PLUID CLONE
TFA Absinthe 1%
TFA Horehound 2%
TFA Kiwi Double 3%
TFA Koolada 1%
LO Marshmallow 2%
TFA Orange Cream 2%
TFA Tangerine 2%

....

FIVE STARS FRUIT 0'S CLONE
TFA Sour 3%
TFA Acetyl Pyrazine 2%
TFA Bavarian Cream 4.5%
TFA Fruit Circles 9%

....

TNT CLONE
TFA Strawberry Ripe 9%
CAP Juicy Peach 4%
CAP Double Apple 7%

....

UNICORN MILK
TPA Bavarian Cream 4%
TPA Cheesecake Graham Crust 5%
TPA Marshmallow 3.5%
TPA Sweet Cream 2%
CAP Sweet Strawberry 4.5%
CAP Vanilla Custard v2 2%

....

BEARD VAPE NO. 5 CLONE
CAP New York Cheesecake 10%
CAP Sweet Strawberry 5%

....

BEARD VAPE NO. 32 CLONE
TPA Banana Nut Bread 1%
FW Bavarian Cream 4%
TPA Brown Sugar Extra 1%
FW Cinnamon Churro 7.5%
FW Cinnamon Roll 7.5%
....

LOOPER CLONE
TPA Bavarian Cream 1%
TPA Berry Crunch 4%
TPA Dairy Milk 2%
TPA Fruit Circles 3%
TPA Strawberry Ripe 5%
28 Day Steep
....

HEISINBERG CLONE
TPA Koolada 1%
TPA Anise Star 2%
TPA Apple Double 1%
TPA Blue Raspberry 4%
TFA Blueberry Candy 8%
TPA Bubblegum 4%
....

DRAGON'S BLOOD
TFA Bavarian Cream 2%
Ethyl Maltol 10% Solution 1%
TFA Vanilla Swirl 3%
TFA Sweet Cream 1%
TFA Strawberry 4%
TFA Dragonfruit 10%
....

DRAGON'S BLOOD TWEAKED
TFA Bavarian Cream 2%
Ethyl Maltol 10% Solution 1%
TFA Vanilla Swirl 2%
TFA Strawberry 6%
TFA Dragon Fruit 10%
....

BETELGEUSE NICOTICKET CLONE
CAP Sweet Strawberry 6%
CAP Golden Pineapple 5%
CAP Raspberry 5%
CAP Sweet Mango 3%
TFA Sweetener 0.50%
65/35 VG/PG
....

SNAKEBITE CLONE
CAP Lemon Sicily 0.50%
TFA Coconut Extra Flavour %
TFA Bavarian Cream Flavour 3%
TFA Green Apple Flavour 5%
....

UNICORN MILK
TFA Dairy Milk 6.31%
TFA Sweet Cream 10.96%
CAP Sweet Strawberry 19.93%
....

COMET TRAILS CLONE
TFA Bavarian Cream 2%
CAP Vanilla Custard v1 2%
TFA Sweet Cream 2%
TFA Cotton Candy 1.5%
TFA Coconut Extra 1.5%
CAP Sweet Guava 8%
....

5 PAWNS CASTLE LONG CLONE
TFA Kentucky Bourbon 2.5%
TFA Coconut Extra 1.5%
TFA Acetyl Pyrazine 1.5%
TFA Toasted Almond 1.5%
TFA Vanillin 1%
TFA Bourbon Vanilla 1%
TFA Brown Sugar Extra 1%
....

CATHERINE THE GRAPE FROM VELVET CLOUD CLONE
FA Blackcurrant 3 %
FA Concord Grape 2%
Ethyl Maltol 10% Solution 1%

....

MILKMAN CLONE
TFA Ethyl Maltol 10% Solution 3%
TFA Strawberry Ripe 7%
TFA Dulce de Leche 2%
TFA Malted Milk 3%
TFA Cheesecake Graham Crust 5%
TFA Whipped Cream 2%
TFA Vanilla Bean Ice Cream 5%
TFA Sweetener 2 %

....

DERAILED SUICIDE BUNNY CLONE
FA Sugar Cookie 15%
CAP Banana 5%
CAP Cinnamon Danish 2%

....

MILKMAN CLONE
TFA Marshmallow 2.04%
TFA Vanilla Cupcake 1.63%
TFA Vanilla Custard 0.82%
TFA Sweetener 4.08%
TFA Whipped Cream 1.63%
CAP Sweet Strawberry 3.27%
TFA Ripe strawberry 4.90%
3 Day Steep

....

ATOMIC CINNACIDE (TASTY VAPOR) CLONE Found By Chris Jungle
CAP Banana 0.5%
TPA Bavarian Cream 2%
TPA Cinnamon Red Hot 10%
TPA Pie Crust 1%
TPA Vanilla Swirl 4%

....

MUFFIN MAN CLONE
FA Fuji Apple 2.75%
FW Cinnamon Roll 5.50%
24 Hour Breathe
7 Day Steep

....

COSMIC FOG MILK & HONEY CLONE Found By Chris Jungle:
TPA Graham Cracker Clear 8%
TPA Marshmallow 3%
TPA Vanilla Swirl 2%
TPA Vanilla Custard 2%
TPA Peanut Butter 1.5%

....

5 PAWNS PERPETUAL CHECK CLONE Found By Chris Jungle:
FA Cinnamon Ceylon 5%
FA Blackcurrant 2%
FA Fresh Fig 0.9%
FA Lemon Sicily 1.25%
FA Catalan Cream 0.75%
FA Vanilla Classic 0.75%
SI Brandy 1.50%
TPA Sweetener 0.5%
Ethyl Maltol 10% Solution 0.25%

....

ANDROMEDA STYLE
TFA Blueberry Wild 6%
TFA Pomegranate 7%
TFA Sweet Cream 3%
14 Day Steep

....

DR.JEKYLL DIGBY'S CLONE
DV Absinthe 6%
TPA French Vanilla 0.3%
TPA Peppermint 0.8%
TPA Sweetener 2.3%

....

CEREAL KILLA 9 SOUTH VAPES CLONE
FA Bergamot 1.5%
FW Yellow Cake 2%
FW Hazelnut 2%
FE Lemon 3%
CAP Lemon Meringue Pie 0.5%
FA Meringue 2%
FA Orange 1%
TFA Sucralose 1%
CAP Sweet Tangerine 1%

···

AMBROSIA ELYSIAN E-LIXIRS CLONE
CAP Cinnamon Danish Swirl v2 12%
TFA Vanilla Cupcake 2%

···

APPLE CINNANA FUZION VAPOR CLONE
TFA Banana Cream 8%
TFA Strawberry Ripe 8%
TFA Apple 6%
TFA Ripe Banana 0.5%
TFA Cinnamon Red Hot 0.5%

···

HALO TRIBECA CLONE
Ethyl Maltol 10% Solution 3%
TFA Acetyl Pyrazine 5% Solution 2%
TFA Graham Cracker 3%
TFA RY4 Double 13%

···

KARMA CREAM MR. GOOD VAPE CLONE
TFA Bavarian Cream 3%
TFA Cheesecake Graham Crust 6%
TFA Graham Cracker 2%
TFA Marshmallow 2%
TFA Strawberry Ripe 6%
CAP Peach & Cream 6%
TFA Sweet Cream 3%
TFA Graham Cracker 2%
TFA Acentyl Pyrazine 1%
Ethyl Maltol 10% Solution 1%
....

MAN FLU CLONE By Don Wave Murphy
CV Honey And Lemon Menthol 15%
CV Menthol Concentrate 1%
CV Absinthe 0.75%
....

KENTUCKY APPLEWOOD VERMILLION RIVER CLONE
TPA Marshmallow 5%
TPA Hazelnut 4%
TPA Original Caramel 3%
TPA Tobacco Blend 2%
LO Apple 2%
....

MADRINA V2 SUICIDE BUNNY CLONE
TFA Cantaloupe 8%
TFA Jackfruit 1%
TFA Watermelon Candy 4%
TFA Bavarian Cream 2%
TPA Honeydew 6%
TPA Sweet Cream 2%
60/40 VG/PG
....

CHARLIE'S CHALK DUST DREAM CREAM CLONE Found By Chris Jungle:
CAP Sweet Tangerine 1%
FW Hazelnut 1%
TPA Graham Cracker Clear 2%
CAP Vanilla Custard v1 12%
FA Fresh Cream 1%
TPA Bavarian Cream 2%

....

BOMBIES A REAL NIGHTMARE CLONE Found By Chris Jungle:
CAP Dutch Chocolate Mint 4.5%
LO Mint Chocolate Chip 2.5%
FA Cookie 2%
TPA Graham Cracker 3%
TPA Mild Black 2.5%
CAP Root Beer 1.5%
TPA Double Chocolate Dark 2%
TPA Coffee 0.5%
TPA Espresso 0.5%
TPA Smooth 0.66%

....

SPACE JAM PLUTO
TPA Honeydew 9%
TPA Bubblegum 4.5%
TPA Peppermint 0.5%

....

MOM'S PINEAPPLE CAKE EPICLOUDS CLONE
CAP Cake Batter 3%
TPA Graham Cracker 3%
CAP New York Cheesecake 2%
TPA Pineapple 2%
CAP Vanilla Custard v1 4%
65/35 VG/PG

....

OMEGA VAPE CHRONOS CLONE Found By Chris Jungle:
FA Butterscotch 3%
FA Bittersweet Chocolate 2%
FA Madagascar Vanilla Classic 3%
FA Marshmallow 5%
FA Meringue 2%

....

COSMIC FOG NUTZ CLONE Found By Chris Jungle:
CAP Sweet Strawberry 3%
TFA Ripe Strawberry 4%
FA Meringue 1%
FA Vienna Cream 2%
FA Almond 2%
FA Caramel 1.5%
CAP Vanilla Custard v1 1%
INA Biscuit 2%
MTS Vape Wizard 2 Drops Per 30ml

....

SUMMER SWEET VELVET CLOUD VAPOR CLONE
CAP Sweet Tea 6%
TFA Raspberry 4%
TFA Lemon 3%
TFA Sweetener 2%
TFA Sour 1%

....

LENOLA CREAM KITE IN CLOUD CLONE
LA Cheesecake 3.5%
Vanilla 10% Solution 2.75%
INW Strawberry 1%
FA Coconut 2%
CAP Vanilla Custard V2 3%
70/30 VG/PG

....

MOON SUGAR MR GOOD VAPE CLONE
CAP Graham Cracker 8%
CAP Sugar Cookie 4%
CAP Caramel 3%
CAP Ethyl Maltol 1-2%

....

THE BELL FROM H4KJUICE CLONE
TFA Citrus Punch 8%
TFA Blueberry Wild 8%
TFA Key Lime 2%
TFA Menthol 1.25%

....

SMURF BALLS BY ZEUS JUICE CLONE
TFA Sweet Cream 10%
LO Blueberry 6%
LO Strawberry 4%

....

THE DUDE ALPHA VAPE CLONE
TFA Juicy Peach 8%
TFA Pineapple 5%
TFA Ethyl Maltol 10% Solution 3%
TFA Mango 2%

....

BEARD VAPE NO. 64 CLONE
CAP Blue Raspberry Cotton Candy 10%
CAP Hibiscus 5%

....

COSMIC FOG SHOCKER CLONE
Citric Acid or Lemon Juice 1Drop Per 5ml
Ethyl Maltol 10% Solution 1%
TFA Sour 0.3%
FW Strawberry Lemonade 10%

....

ALICE IN VAPELAND WHITE RABBIT CLONE
TFA French Vanilla 6%
TFA Marshmallow 6%
TFA Whipped Cream 4%
TFA Sweet Cream 2%
TFA Coconut 2%

....

5 PAWNS 5TH RANK CLONE
TPA Caramel Original 3%
TPA Champagne 3%
TPA Horehound 4%
TPA Key Lime 1%
TPA Menthol 0.5%
TPA Smooth 1%
TPA Sweet Cream 4%
TPA Sweetener 1%
TPA Toasted Almond 1%
TPA Vanilla Bean Ice Cream 6%

....

CUTTWOOD BOSS RESERVE CLONE
TFA Graham Cracker Clear 3.3%
TFA Caramel Original 3.3%
FW Captain Crunch 3%
TFA Peanut Butter 3.3%
TFA Vanilla Swirl 2%
TFA Vanilla Custard 4%
TFA Banana Cream 10%
TFA Cotton Candy 1%

....

CUTTWOOD SUGAR BEAR/SUGAR DRIZZLE CLONE
CAP Cinnamon Danish Swirl 4.8%
CAP Cinnamon Roll 8%
TFA Sugar Cookie 3.2%
Ethyl Maltol 10% Solution 1%
24 Hour Breathe
21 Day Steep

....

SPACE JAM ECLIPSE CLONE
TFA Western 10%
CAP Vanilla Custard v1 8%
CAP Marshmallow 5%

....

5 PAWNS PERPETUAL CHECK CLONE
FA Cinnamon Ceylon 5%
FA Blackcurrant 2%
FA Fresh Fig 0.9%
FA Lemon Sicily 1.25%
FA Catalan Cream 0.75%
FA Vanilla Classic 0.75%
SI Brandy 1.5%
TFA Sweetener 0.5%
TFA Ethyl Maltol 10% Solution 0.25%
....

TIME BOMB TNT CLONE
TFA Strawberry Ripe 9%
CAP Juicy Peach 4%
CAP Double Apple 7%
....

VAPOUR TRAILS SASQUATCH CLONE
TFA Blueberry Wild 8%
TFA Hazelnut 2%
CAP Sweet Cream 1.5%
TFA Bavarian Cream2%
....

Flavour	Steeping Time
Mother's Milk Clone	28 Days
Milkman Clone	3 Days
Muffin Man Clone	7 Days
Andromeda Style	14 Days
Sugar Drizzle Clone	21 Days

Appendix 1 - Mixing Suppliers

PG, VG, NICOTINE, AND CONCENTRATE SUPPLIERS
http://www.valiant2vape.co.uk/
http://www.darkstarvapour.co.uk/
https://www.chefsvapour.co.uk/25-concentrates
http://www.justvape247.com/branded-concentrates-91-c.asp
http://www.astorwi.co.uk/?product=99
www.vapable.com
http://thee-cigshop.co.uk/DIY
http://decadentvapours.com/product-category/connoisseur-range/flavours/
http://www.flavourart.co.uk/
http://www.totallywicked-eliquid.co.uk/e-liquid/mix-your-own-e-liquid/
flavour-concentrates.html
http://www.thealchemistscupboard.co.uk/product/capella
http://www.fsecig.com/mix.../eliquid-flavour-concentrates/
http://www.cloud9vaping.co.uk/FL10
http://www.vapedomain.co.uk/
http://www.vampirevape.co.uk/.../flavour-concentrates/
http://piratesvape.uk/
http://www.liberty-flights.co.uk/products.asp
https://bigjuiceuk.co.uk
http://www.leisureliquids.com/?m=no
Lubrisolve:
T +44(0) 1458-259479
M +44(0) 7831-189311
e-mail: enquiries@lubrisolve.co.uk

EQUIPMENT
http://www.bottles4us.co.uk/
https://www.ibottles.co.uk/
http://www.wizardvapes.co.uk/
https://www.creamsupplies.co.uk/index.php?act=viewCat&catId=365

Appendix 2 - Single Flavour Concentrates

(Credit Goes To Danial Carcas)

Single flavours and where they are from % is how much % of flavour to base

✔ means mixed by myself and tastes good

X means tasted bad

The number at the end is steep time (DAYS)

All PG/VG Ratio for these are 40/60

If you want a higher VG ratio then you may have to up the percentage and vice versa

ALL MIXES ARE LEFT OPEN TO AIR FOR 24HRS

Vampire Vapes:

Heisenberg	12% ✔	2
Pinkman	12% ✔	2
Vamp Toes	12% ✔	2
Attraction	12% ✔	2
Bat Juice	12% ✔	2

Vape Domain:

Dragons Blood	15% ✔	2
Strawberry Lime Kopparberg	12% ✔	3
Blue Slush	12% ✔	2
Lilt	14% ✔	3
Wham Bar	12% ✔	2
Millions	12% ✔	2
Mixed Fruit Kopparberg	12% ✔	2

Kandi Head:

Blueberry Lemonade	12% ✔	2
Blackcurrant Liq	10% ✔	X

Flavour West:

Green Goblin	13%	✔	2
Beetle Juice	13%	✔	2
Jungle Juice	13%	✔	2
Cherry Crush	12%	✔	3
Cream Soda	12%	✔	X
Mt Dew	12%	✔	2
Skittles	12%	✔	2
Unicorn Vomit	12%	✔	7-10
Tiki Roar	12%	✔	5
Watermelon Candy	12%	✔	3
Apple Jacks	10%	✔	9

One-On-One:

Pink Lemonade	13%	✔	2
Strawberry Lemonade	14%	✔	2
Blueberry Yoghurt	13%	✔	14
Malted Milk	12%	✔	X
Cocopops	12%	✔	14 X
Orange Sherbet Ice Cream	12%	✔	4
Apple Candy	12%	✔	2
Gummy Fish Candy	12%	✔	2

The Perfume Apprentice:

Berry Crunch	12%	✔	14
Pear Candy	12%	✔	2
Silly Rabbit	12%	✔	9
Fruit Circles	12%	✔	9
Hawaiian Punch	14%	✔	2

Mount Baker:

Raspberry Lemonade	12%	✔	2
Blue Moo	12%	✔	14
Fruity Hoops	10%	✔	9

Chefs Vapor:

Banana Martini	10%	✔
Peach Martini	10%	✔
Mango Martini	10%	✔

Appendix 3 - Guide to Average Percentages

FOR BRANDED CONCENTRATES

The following percentages are a guideline only sourced from user info and maker recommendations personal taste and mixing ratios play a great part.

CAPELLA

....

Amaretto = 6%To 8%
Apple Pie = 7% To 9%
Banana = 17% To 21%
Blueberry = 16% To 20%
Banana Split =7% To 9%
Blueberry = 16% To 20%
Blueberry Cinnamon Crumble 8% To 12%
Blue Raspberry Cotton Candy 8% To 12%
Boston Cream Pie =15% To 20%
Bull Horn = 9% To 12%
Cappuccino = 10%To 12%
Cherry Cola =14% To 16%
Choc Glazed Doughnut = 8% To 11%
Chocolate Fudge Brownie =8% To 11%
Chocolate Raspberry =18% To 20%
Cranberry = 10% To 12%
Double Chocolate Mint = 9% To 11%
Egg Nog = 8% To 10%
Hot Cocoa = 7% To 10%
Irish Cream = 6% To 8%
Popcorn = 10 To 12%
Pineapple And Cream 8% To 11%
Sweet Guava = 8% To 10%
Sweet Tangerine = 13% To 16%
Vanilla Cupcake = 7% To 10%
Vanilla Custard = 12% To 14%

DECADENT VAPOURS

Absinthe = 7% To 8%
American Red = 9% To 12%
Apple = 14% To 16%
Banana = 9% To 11%
Black Cherry = 9% To 11%
Blackcurrant = 9% To 11%
Caramel 10% To 14%
Cherry Ice = 11% To 13%
Choc Caramel = 12% To 15%
Coconut Ice = 10% To 12%
Cola Kick = 10% To 12%
Dy3 = 15%
Dy4 = 15%
Gingerbread =11% To 14%
Line Zinger = 11% To 14%
Parma Violet = 10% To 12%
Raspberry = 12% To 14%

FLAVOURART

Almond = 2% To 5%
Anise = 4% T0 6%
Apple = 4% To 6%
Apricot = 3% To 6%
Banana = 4% To 7%
Beer = 5%
Bilberry = 2% To 4%
Black Cherry = 4% To 6%
Black Tea = 4% To 6%
Blackberry = 3% To 5%
Blackcurrant = 3% To 5%
Brandy = 2% To 4%
Butterscotch = 3% To 5%
Cappuccino = 4% To 5%
Caramel = 4% To 6%
Catalan Cream = 4% To 6%
Cherry = 6% To 8%
Chocolate = 5% To 7%
Cinnamon =4% To 5%
Citrus Mix = 4% To 8%
Cocoa = 4% To 6%

Vaping Home Brewers Handbook

Coconut = 6% To 9%
Coffee Espresso = 2.5% To 4.5%
Cola = 4% To 7%
Cookie = 3.5% To 5.5%
Cream Fresh = 4%
Cream Whipped = 4%
Custard = 5% To 7%
Fig = 4% To 5%
Forest Fruit = 4% To 7%
Green Tea = 3% To 4%
Guava = 3% To 5%
Hazelnut =3% To 5%
Honey = 4% To 6%
Irish Cream = 3% To 4%
Kiwi = 4% To 5%
Liquorice = 4% To 5%
Cold Pressed Lime = 4%
Lime Tahiti = 3% To 4%
Lychee = 4% To 6%
Mad Fruit = 5%
Mandarin = 6%
Mango = 5% To 8%
Marshmallow = 4% To 5%
Menthol Arctic = 2% To 4%
Nut Mix = 3%
Orange = 5% To 6%
Passion Fruit = 4% To 5%
Peach = 4% To 5%
Peanut = 3% To 5%
Pear = 4% To 7%
Peppermint = 3% To 5%
Pineapple = 5% To 9%
Pomegranate = 3% To 4%
Raspberry = 6% To 9%
Red Bull = 3% To 5%
Spearmint = 5% To 6%
Strawberry = 2% To 3.5%
Tiramisu = 4% To 6%
Tutti Frutti = 2% To 4%
Vanilla Bourbon = 5% To 8%
Walnut = 4% To 6%
Whiskey = 3% To 4%

FLAVOURWEST

American Coke = 12% To 15%
Apricot = 14% To 17%
Banana = 12% To 15%
Banana Foster = 12% To 15%
Banana Nut Bread = 9% To 11 %
Black Liquorice = 11% To 13%
Black Cherry = 16% To 18%
Bubble Gum = 14% To 16%
Butter Rum = 10% To 13%
Butter Popcorn = 10% To 13%
Cake Yellow = 14% To 16%
Cappuccino = 11% To 14%
Caramel Candy = 14% To 16%
Cinnamon Red Hot = 6% To 8%
Cinnamon Roll = 14% To 16%
Coconut Cream Pie = 12% To 15%
Coffee = 9% To 11%
Cookies And Cream = 16% To 20%
Cotton Candy = 14% To 16 %
Cream Soda = 13% To 15%
Double Apple = 15% To 17%
Doublemint Gum = 14% To 16%
Ecto Cooler = 15% To 18%
Guava = 11% To 14%
Gummy Bear = 9% To 11%
Hazelnut = 12% To 15%
Jungle Juice = 12% To 14%
Key Lime = 15% To 20%
Lemonade = 9% To 11%
0Range = 15% To 17%
Orange Dream Bar = 14% To 16%
Peach = 13% To 16%
Peanut Butter = 15% To 18%
Pineapple = 14% To 16%
Pink Champagne = 13% To 15%
Plumb = 13% To 15%
Ruby Red Grapefruit = 13% To 15%
Snickers Type = 14% To 16%
Swiss Cherry = 12% To 15%
Tangerine = 15% To 18%
Tropical Punch = 14% To 16%

Vanilla Custard = 14% To 16%
Waffle = 18% To 20%
White Chocolate = 15% To 18%

INAWERA FLAVOURS

Banana = 4% To 6%
Blackberry = 4% To 6%
Cappuccino = 4% To 6%
Cola = 3% To 5%
Cool Mint = 3% To 4%
Hazelnut = 3% To 5%
Honey = 3% To 4%
Grape = 3% To 4%
Lemon = 3% To 4%
Milk Chocolate = 5% To 8%
Mint = 3% To 5%
Nougat = 6% To 8%
Orange = 3.5% To 4.5%
Peanut = 3% To 5%
Plum = 4% To 5%
Raspberry = 3% To 5%
Two Apples = 4% To 6%
Lemon = 4% To 6%

THE PERFUMERS APPRENTICE

Absinthe = 5% To 8%
Apple = 12% To 14%
Banana Cream = 15% To 20%
Blackberry = 14% To 16%
Black Cherry = 9% To 12%
Caramel Original = 16% To 20%
Caramel Candy = 15% To 18%
Chai Tea = 8% To 10%
Cinnamon Danish = 8% To 10%
Coffee - 4% To 7%
Creme De Mint = 5% To 7%
Dragonfruit = 9% To 11%
Double Chocolate = 4% To 6%
French Vanilla = 7% To 10%
Gingerbread = 8% To 11%
Granny Smith = 7% To 9%

Damien Smy

Green Tea = 5% To 7%
Hazelnut = 9% To 11%
Honey = 6.5% To 8.5%
Lemon = 9% To 11%
Mary Jane = 14% To 16%
Milk Chocolate = 8% To 11%
Mocha = 5% To 7%
Passion Fruit =9% To 12%
Pineapple = 11% To 13%
Pina Colada = 5% To 6%
Popcorn = 14% To 16%
Raspberry = 11% To 14%
Ripe Banana =14% To 16%
Ry4 = 13% To 15%
Strawberry And Cream = 9% To 12%
Waffel = 10% To 14%

TASTY PUFF

....

Awesome Apple = 2% To 4%
Blueberry Thrill = 3.5% To 5%
California Orange = 2% To 3%
Chick Magnet Cherry = 4% To 4%
Chumpy Chocolate = 4% To 5%
Chronic Hypnotic = 4% To 5%
Convicted Melon (Melone) = 4% To 6%
Crazy Coconut = 2% To 4%
Electric Banana = 4% To 6%
Flower Power = 3% To 4%
Jungle Juice = 4% To 6%
Mango Tango = 4% To 5%
Mr Bubble = 4% To 6%
Pimpy Fresh Peach = 4% To 6%
Purple Haze = 3% To 4%
Rasta Rootbeer = 3% To 4%
Rippin' Raspberry = 4% To 6%
Silly Strawberry = 3% To 5%
Sinful Cinnamon = 4% To 5%
Spiffy Spearmint = 3% To 4%
Toke A Cola = 5% To 6%

TOTALLY WICKED GOLD

Blue Hawaii = 5% To 7%
Ice Menthol = 3% To 4%
Iron Brewed = 3% To 4%

Appendix 4 - Common Abbreviations

FOR CONCENTRATE MANUFACTURERS

CAP = Capella
INA/INW =Inawera
TPA/TFA = The Perfumers Apprentice/The Flavourers Apprentice
FA = Flavourart
FW = Flavourwest
DV = Decadant Vapours
M+P = Moms and Pops
OOO = One-on-One Flavours
PSV/PS = Pink Spot Vapours
TP = Tasty Puff
CK = Classikool
TWG = Totally Wicked Gold
KH = Kandi-hed
LO/LA = Lor Ann
FLV = Flavourah
CCW = Cup Cake World
CV/CC/CHC = Chef's Vapour Own/Chefs Choice
VV = Vampire Vapes
CVR - Chef's Rebranded
JF - Juice Factory
TJ - T-Juice
CJ - Ciggy Juice
FJ - Flavour Junkie
NF - Nature's Flavours
TDM - Tino D'Milano
VBL - Vapeable
HS - Hangsen
CI - Cuts Ice
LL - Leisure Liquids
BJ - Big Juice
FE - Flavour Express
VD - Vape Domain
SI - Signature
MB - Mount Baker

Appendix 5 - Steeping

WHAT IS STEEPING?
Steeping is the process of allowing the flavours to mix, and combine to give the best possible taste.

HOW DO YOU STEEP LIQUIDS?
The best possible steeping method to leave a juice in a room temperature, dark place. This reduces the amount the nicotine from oxidising, and changing the colour of the juice. Some juices will darken over time, even without nicotine.

There are many methods people will attempt to use to speed steep their juices, such as using a slow cooker, a saucepan of water, a microwave, USB cup warmers, and possibly others we have not yet encountered. There may be some truth to these, however, time is the best method out there.

If you do decide to try one of the heating methods, it is suggested that you leave the nicotine out of the juice until you have finished, as you will either break the nicotine down, or evaporate it, making it pointless having put it in, in the first place.

THERE ARE TWO MAJOR PROCESSES INVOLVED IN STEEPING E-LIQUID
1. Removal of volatile components by evaporation and degasification
This process would include the removal of alcohol but is not restricted to alcohol, there are other volatile components used in the production of flavour concentrates that generally give off an astringent or chemical odour. These process requires access to the atmosphere hence the need to remove tops from bottles.

1a Evaporation – This is the same process as used in cooking to remove alcohol from wine.

1b Degasification – This is the same process as letting a fizzy drink go flat

Both of these processes are accelerated by heat and increased surface area. This is a critical first step many e-Liquids are hideous and un-vapeable before this process. Without acceleration this can take a week or longer due to the viscosity of the liquid.

2. The Development Of Complex Flavour Molecules.
Over time some e-Liquids especially custard/caramel or desert flavours darken. From observation this cannot be oxidation as it oc-curs uniformly through the liquid and does not require agitation of the liquid to occur. It also cannot be caramelisation as this does not occur below 110°C.

MAILLARD REACTION - COLOUR AND FLAVOUR

What seems to be happening is a Maillard reaction commonly experi-enced by most people every day. The browning of bread, toast and potato chips, these are high temperature examples. Medium tempera-ture examples creating Dulce de Leche and condensed milk.

Mallard reactions also occur at lower temperatures and contribute to the ageing of wine and Balsamic Vinegar.

Maillard reactions get exponentially slower as they progress. This fits in with our observations of steeping e-Liquid, a golden colour may be observed in a couple of days however the full desired flavour and colour may take 4-6 weeks to develop. The Maillard reactions will continue to progress over time, hence those almost black bottles of e-Liquid that are found at the back of a draw.

The degree of colour change is dependent on the type of flavours present and the presence of Nicotine. Some flavours wont change at all these are often referred to as shake and vape liquids. This mirrors the culinary world, you never see matured lemonade being sold.

ACCELERATING THE STEEPING PROCESS. REMOVAL OF VOLATILE COMPONENTS BY EVAPORATION AND DE-GASIFICATION

A. Taking the top off the bottle.
B. Shaking the bottle (Helps)
C. Stirring (Helps)
D. Whisking (Very effective)
E. Blending to a foam (Super Effective)
F. Ultrasonic degasification (Super Effective)

NOTES

NOTES